W9-BRY-072

Presented by:

_____

To:

_____

Date:

_____

Occasion:

_____

The Golden
Thread of Life

"99 Words to Live By"

A series of fine gift books that presents inspirational words by renowned authors and captivating thinkers. Thought-provoking proverbs from many peoples and traditions complete each volume's collection.

"99 Words to Live By" explores topics that have moved and will continue to move people's hearts. Perfect for daily reflection as well as moments of relax.

The Golden
Thread of Life

99 Sayings
on Love

edited by
Gabrielle Hartl

New City Press

Published in the United States by New City Press
202 Cardinal Rd., Hyde Park, NY 12538
©2003 New City Press (English translation)

Translated by the NCP editorial staff
from the original German edition
Wo Liebe sich freut, ist ein Fest
©1997 Verlag Neue Stadt, Munich.

Cover picture: Vincent van Gogh,
Vase with lilacs, daisies and anemones (detail)

Library of Congress Cataloging-in-Publication Data:

Wo Liebe sich freut, ist ein Fest. English
  The golden thread of life : 99 sayings on love / edited by
    Gabrielle Hartl.
    p. cm. (99 words to live by)
ISBN 1-56548-182-8
  1. Love--Quotations, maxims, etc. I. Hartl, Gabrielle. II.
    Title. III. Series.

PN6093.L6W613 2003

                                    2003044518

Printed in Canada

Ask anyone for the most beautiful word in their language. "Love" will be the most likely response.

"The first happy memory of a child is the realization that he or she is loved," says John Bosco. The word "love" usually calls forth from us the most sublime sentiments: longing, pain and profound joy. Love is present in so many forms: between parents and children, among friends, between husband and wife; it sustains our care for neighbor and for the poor.

All forms of love come from the same root and have the same goal, the same power; a power, which supports, spurns and strengthens. In fact, without love there would be no life on this planet of ours, and no happiness either.

Love can be lived and experienced to the full, but hardly put into words ... not even into 99 Words...

The Editor

Love
is like the moon.
When it doesn't wax
it wanes.

Vicomte de Segur

In the kingdom of love
there are no plains.
You either ascend
or you descend.

Fulton J. Sheen

Learning and loving
are two things
we should
never be done with.

Josef Bernhart

Love

is the spirit
that gives life to all things.

Tschu-Li

Only love
can give meaning
to our lives.
This means
that the more we grow
in our ability to love
and to give of ourselves,
the more meaningful
our lives will be.

Hermann Hesse

Love
is the ultimate purpose
of history
and the final word
of the universe.

Novalis

Everything
in this world
is in a relationship of love.
But we have to live love
to discover
the golden thread
that binds all created beings
to one another.

Chiara Lubich

We are truly human
inasmuch as we love.

Alfred Delp

The sum total
of our life
is made up
of those hours
in which we have loved.

Wilhelm Busch

All meaning
in life
is fulfilled
where love reigns.

Dietrich Bonhoeffer

When you have a thousand reasons for living, when you never feel lonely, and upon awakening feel like singing; when everything is meaningful — from the rocks on the road to the stars in the sky, from the lazy lizard to the fish that reign the ocean — when you can listen to the wind and hear the silence, then rejoice:
Love is at your side,
it is your travel companion,
your sister.

Helder Camara

Love

and do what you wish!
Are you silent?
Be silent out of love.
Do you have to reprove
a neighbor?
Reprove out of love.
Do you have to wait?
Wait out of love.
In the depths of your heart
have only the root of love;
from this root
only good things
can come.

Augustine of Hippo

At the end of life,
we will be judged
only by love.

From the rule of Taizé

A drop of love
is worth more
than a sea
of good will and reason.

Blaise Pascal

Now I will show you the way
which surpasses all others:

If I speak with human
and angelic tongues,
but do not have love,
I am a noisy gong,
a clanging cymbal.
If I have the gift of prophecy
and know all mysteries,
if I have faith great enough
to move mountains,
but have not love,
I am nothing.

Paul to the Corinthians

Nothing
in our struggles can harm us
— as long as we
don't lose love.

Roger Schütz of Taizé

Love is the only thing
that grows in us
as we freely give of it.

Ricarda Huch

The essence of love
is self-giving.

Edith Stein

In this, possibly,
lies the greatest love:
to nourish our neighbor
with all that we are ourselves.

Romano Guardini

You cannot give love
if you don't have it.
And you only have it
if you give it.

Augustine of Hippo

The best anyone can *do*
for another
is always what he *is*
for the other.

Adalbert Stifter

This is the innermost
and outermost quality
of both God and man:
to not merely *give* gifts
to one another
but to *be* gifts
for one another.

Klaus Hemmerle

Love
gives nothing but itself,
and takes nothing
but what comes from itself.
Love does not possess
and cannot be possessed.
When you love, don't say
"God is in my heart";
rather say "I am in God's heart."
And don't think
you can guide love's course;
because love,
if you are worthy of it,
will guide yours.

Kahlil Gibran

Faithfulness
is a proof of love.
But forgiveness
is its fulfillment.

Werner Bergengruen

24

Should you have faults, I will understand. Love is not to form an image in one's soul and attribute to it all perfections. Love is rather to love all human beings just as we find them and, should they have weaknesses, to welcome them anyway, with a heart full of love.

Charlotte, his wife,
to Friedrich Schiller

Lovers
thrive on forgiveness.

Manfred Hausmann

Love
that is not
continually renewed,
continually dies.

Kahlil Gibran

Our love
is most intense
in silence.

Charles de Foucauld

The more we love another,
the less words we need
to express it.

Annette von Droste-Hulshoff

Where love cannot walk,
it will crawl.

From England

Love

is a powerful force;
it is the only force
in this world
that cannot be overcome.

Fjodor M. Dostojewski

Omnia vincit amor:
Love conquers all.

Virgil

Love is capable of all;
it can accomplish
many things
that uselessly tire
and wear out the one
who does not have love.

Charles de Foucauld

Nothing is difficult
for the one who loves.
No fatigue is too much
for the one who is filled
with longing.

Hieronymus

Love is proven successful
in the works it does,
and in the obstacles
it overcomes.

Augustine of Hippo

The final lesson of history
could be summed up
in three words:
love one another.

Morton Kelsey

Being ready
to endure the other
may be our last chance
to reach him or her
with our love.

Dieter Emeis

Power without love
is reckless and abusive
and love without power
is sentimental and anemic.

Martin Luther King

If we deny
the reality of both
divine and human love,
we are not dealing
honestly with the universe
in which we live
— we are blind
to the core of reality.

Morton Kelsey

Mighty waters
cannot extinguish love;
strong streams cannot
carry it away;
and should someone
offer all the possessions
of his household
so as to acquire love,
we would only despise him.

From the Song of Love

Love is patient;
love is kind.
Love is not jealous,
it does not put on airs,
it is not snobbish.
Love is never rude,
it is not self-seeking,
it is not prone to anger,
neither does it brood
over injuries.
Love does not rejoice
in what is wrong
but rejoices with the truth.
Love forebears all,
believes all,
hopes all,
endures all.

Paul to the Corinthians

A love
that does not wish
to be constant,
is not strong enough.

Peter Rosegger

Love

is like our daily bread:
always the same,
yet always different.

Sigrid Undset

What, my heart,
are you waiting for?
If you want to love
you can begin right away.

John of the Cross

Where there is no love,
bring love,
and you will find love.

John of the Cross

The world belongs
to the one who loves
and can show it.

The Curate of Ars

There is much coldness
among people,
because we don't dare
to show ourselves
as cordial as we really are.

Albert Schweitzer

Our heart
cannot endure
love for humanity,
if it does not have
people it loves.

Friedrich Holderlin

Here
is the greatest sin
of our time:
abstract love
for people....
It is too easy.

Tolstoi

Love needs to
express itself concretely.
When it finds no way to do so,
it becomes meaningless
and it suffocates.

Paulo E. Arns

Without love
we are a burden
even to ourselves.
With love,
we become a support
for one another.

Augustine of Hippo

Who loves another,
accepts that person
just as he or she is,
has been, and will be.

Michel Quoist

Love
has the power to transform.

Stefan Andres

As far as the eye can see
love is the only
creative principle
that we know.

Gertrud von Le Fort

Where love
is born anew
life is born anew.

Vincent van Gogh

Where
something is done
out of true love,
we are treading
on holy ground.

Johannes Bours

A neighborhood that I had shunned for years, overnight became a second home to me because a person I held dear moved in.

It was as if that person's window shone with a new light, brightening everything.

Walter Benjamin

We dream
of finding a person
who can be
entirely one with us.
While this dream
won't come true
we don't
dream it in vain.
The one who does not
dream it, however,
has known nothing
of true love.

Friedrich Georg Junger

Love asks for everything,
and justly so.
It is what I feel
concerning you,
and you concerning me.

Ludwig van Beethoven

Love does not mean
looking one another
in the eyes,
but looking together
in the same direction.

Antoine de Saint-Exupéry

Love is a gift
and it is given freely.
Love gives of itself
without wanting to receive
anything in return.
The key to life
bears the name "love."

Igino Giordani

Love is not
the embrace of a body
but rather a total gift
of ourselves to a person
whom we love
as God loves us.

Carlo Carretto

Lovers embrace
what exists between them,
rather than each other.

Kahlil Gibran

Isn't it beautiful
to think that so many people
are holy in the eyes of those
who love them?

Christian Morgenstern

To love others
means to see them
as God meant them to be.

Fjodor M. Dostojewski

To love
another person
means to be the one
who sees a miracle,
invisible to everyone else.

François Mauriac

Who loves,
always finds
in the other person
a reason for admiration.

Roger Schütz of Taizé

We cannot explain
why we love someone.
We simply love them.
This is what is amazing,
adventurous,
and breathtaking:
we cannot come to terms
with the people we love,
precisely because
we love them
and for as long
as we love them.

Max Frisch

Love creates the space
where the other
can be oneself.

Romano Guardini

We don't truly love others
unless we take them
as they are.

From Africa

True love begins
where we expect
nothing in return.

Antoine de Saint-Exupéry

The one whom I love
told me that he needs me.
This is why I guard myself,
watch where I am going,
and worry that even
a rain drop may harm me.

Bertold Brecht

True love warms but does not burn.

Flemish

To love means:
to seek the other's happiness.

John Bosco

Rabbi Mosche Leib told this story: How we should love others I learned from a farmer. He was sitting in a pub together with others. For a long time he was silent, just as everyone else. But when the wine had moved his heart, he asked his neighbor: "Tell me, do you love me or do you not love me?" That one replied, "I love you very much." He, however, retorted, "You say, I love you, but you don't know what I am in need of. If you would truly love me, you would know." The other man did not know how to respond, and the farmer who had started the conversation fell silent again as well.

But I understood: This is what loving other means, to feel what others need and to share their pain.

Martin Buber

Love wants nothing
from the other
but wants everything
for the other.

Dietrich Bonhoeffer

Ever since I love you,
I am truly myself
when I am no longer
only myself.

From Japan

Love means this:
When you suffer,
I feel the pain.

Abbé Pierre

You and I: we are one.
I cannot hurt you
without hurting myself.

Mahatma Gandhi

In love, there is no fear.
Rather, true love
expels fear.

From the First Letter of John

The soul in love is gentle, humble, mild-mannered and patient (John of the Cross).

Yes, this is so because she is in love. She lives in fullness, and nothing disturbs her.

She is well disposed toward others because, knowing that she is loved, she does not need to think of herself.

She is patient because she is so fulfilled that she does not need to hurry to reach another goal.

Chiara Lubich

To live means to love,
and to love
means to take risks.

Henri Boulad

Love,
and nothing but love,
brings happiness.
The one
who knows how to love
is happy.

Hermann Hesse

Happiness,
all happiness,
lies in this:
to love and to know
that I am loved.

Chiara Lubich

The one who loves,
lives there where he loves,
not there where he lives.

Augustine of Hippo

The one who loves, gives,
and gives incessantly.
And within, he or she
has a fullness
that never ends.

Chiara Lubich

The affection, the spontaneous love we feel for some people give us the measure of love we should have for all those we meet.

Madeleine Delbrel

The measure of love
is love without measure.

Francis de Sales

We are called
to exaggerate in loving.

Paul VI

Love is the first
and original gift.
Whatever else
we may have received,
without having merited it,
becomes a gift
only through love.

Josef Pieper

God's greatest gift to man
is the power to love.
Never will it be taken away
from the blessed soul
who loves.

Kahlil Gibran

I give you
a new commandment:
love one another.
Just as I have loved you,
so you should love
one another.

Jesus Christ

When we love selflessly,
we are but a stone's throw
away from heaven.

Saying from Mount Athos

The one
who does good
dwells at the temple's gate;
the one who loves,
enters its sanctuary.

Rabindranath Tagore

The ones
who know God best
are the ones who love;
to these the theologian
should listen.

Hans Urs von Balthasar

Power
we can obtain
through knowledge;
but fulfillment
we will only reach
through love.

Rabindranath Tagore

The one
who wants to reach
the summit of wisdom
needs to ascend
the summit of love.
Because no one is perfect
in knowledge
who is not perfect
in love.

Rhabanus Maurus

Have no debt
with anyone;
be debtors only in love.
The one who loves
one's neighbor
has fulfilled the law.

Paul to the Corinthians

Love
knows no end.

Paul to the Corinthians

"99 Words To Live By"

Also available now:

Blessed Are the Peacemakers
99 Sayings on Peace
ISBN 1-56548-183-6, 112 pp., hardcover

In preparation:

Sunshine
On Our Way
99 Sayings on Friendship
(January 2004)

Organizations and Corporations

This title is available at special quantity discounts for bulk purchases for sales promotions, premiums, or fundraising.
For information call or write:

New City Press, Marketing Dept.
202 Cardinal Rd.
Hyde Park, NY 12538.
Tel: 1-800-462-5980;
1-845-229-0335
Fax: 1-845-229-0351
info@newcitypress.com

"99 Words To Live By"

Future volumes include:

99 Sayings on ...
Christmas
Time
The Desert
Thankfulness
Silence
Hope

99 Sayings by ...
Mother Teresa
Mahatma Gandhi
Chiara Lubich
Martin Buber
Edith Stein
John XXIII
Simone Weil
Dag Hammarskjold